To Ade,

Thank you for !

Witness

Jonathan Kinsman

Jonathan Kinsman

Burning Eye

BurningEyeBooks
Never Knowingly
Mainstream

LOTTERY FUNDED

Supported using public funding by
**ARTS COUNCIL
ENGLAND**

This edition published by Burning Eye Books 2020

www.burningeye.co.uk
@burningeyebooks

Burning Eye Books
15 West Hill, Portishead, BS20 6LG

ISBN 978-1-911570-82-0

Jonathan Kinsman (he/they) is a trans poet from Manchester. Raised Church of England and with a background in theological study, he lives his life marrying his spirituality with his queer identity. As well as being founding editor of Riggwelter Press and associate editor of Three Drops From A Cauldron, he is also a multiple slam finalist. His debut pamphlet & was joint-winner of the Indigo Dreams Pamphlet Prize 2017.

*in loving memory of john and pauline early and ron cassidy,
who taught me god.*

contents

andrew

'he came as a witness to testify to the light.'

john 1:7

in galilee, some grey and dirty town
      long forgot by parliament, where the air
stinks like rotting fish, like waters going stagnant,
      everyone is plotting their escape

and you are no exception. jonah's wayward kid,
      hair in his face and holes in his hoodie sleeves,
trailing after some pretentious fucking nickname,
      hanging on his every word.

all those freaks and weirdos, you among them,
      loitering on the docks. seagulls, feral cats.
you scare the neighbourhood watch doing nothing.
      and baptist's saying *something's gotta give.*

there's more than this. and you make yourself believe him,
      even if on your last day of school you walked out
from the exam hall onto your dad's ancient, grubby trawler,
      up to your elbows in muck and guts,

simon by your side muttering *get your head outta the clouds.*
      grow the fuck up. and still you resist,
keep your hair long, drink cheap wine in the park at midnight,
      waiting, always waiting

until that glorious afternoon the cloud cover breaks,
      and baptist is the first in the water,
splashing, pouring it over your heads with childish glee,
      a stranger slipping amongst you, unnoticed,

why don't we just go? there's no one stopping us.
      just get on a bus and get gone –
met with sheepish mumbling. but you can't bear it.
      another day just like the last. the sun gone in for good.

take me. i'll come. rising from your throat unbidden,
            things can't stay this way. i can't stay this way.
and suddenly your dripping feet are flying down the road
            and you are screaming at the top of your lungs

you gotta hear this. you've all gotta hear this.

simon the zealot

'for it is written, vengeance is mine, i will repay.'
romans 12:19

you say *give me a gun. i'll shoot my way out.* but nobody does
when you're caught in the trap and from land and sky comes
everything you'd prayed might pass over, hit some other city –
anywhere with thicker walls, somebody who could only speak
and stop the shaking, set the dust back on the ground again.

but aleppo is just baghdad is just kabul is just gaza where they
forecast plague and scourge in the weather segments. hail and
fire moving through to tuesday evening when you begin to
see blackouts sweeping in from the east; blood in the water,
smeared over the doorframes where they'd told you to stand.

you're saying *if i'd had a gun. if there'd only been someone.*
but there wasn't. so you cross a sea the way the godless do,
ready to drown – the bread of europe dirt in your mouth, the
promised land miles of tents and tarpaulins and ringing in your
ears the shouts of greed: cry thief, cry migrant, cry demons
come climbing up those chalk white cliffs.

so when god walks amongst you in those ramshackle streets,
reconstitutes the dust of shattered bones, fills each open,
empty palm, whispers *blessed is every last one*, you say
give me a gun, lord.

give me strength enough to lift a ceiling,
give me a staff to part an ocean, give me a voice
louder than falling bombs and i am yours, god.
what i am capable of, when you are with me,
some call zealous and others terror –
but give me a gun, god.
give me a fighting chance.

he holds you while your body shakes, while you pound your
fists against the ground like you could beat the devil back to

hell. in your mind, the gun in your hands, your finger trembling
over the trigger you cannot pull when your eyes meet a boy's
over its barrel and recognise that same spark of fury deep in
their darkness, that same quake of fear in his hands.

and god is saying, *simon, come with me, simon,*
put down your gun.
there's a war yet to be won.

matthew

'for i have come to call not the righteous but sinners.'
matthew 9:13

when you meet god, he's on the open mic
of the seediest bar in town and you're slamming
down the pornstar martinis, politely declining
something quick and dirty in the nearest alley.

you didn't come here for a cheap fuck; you just
didn't want to see the twats you work with.

because on the weekends you don't pretend –
even if you're still blond-haired and blue-eyed,
you tell that that your first name's really levi
and you wanted to do your parents proud.

so much money spent on a public schoolboy
education; on ppe at cambridge, all so you could

do something with mortgages, some shit
with stocks, with acquisitions and mergers and bite
your tongue when your colleagues debate back
and forth on eugenics, laugh along when

jew is the punchline. at this bar everyone hates you,
but at least you don't hate them and when

god calls you by your name, you pull up an extra stool.
you let him take a seat, turn to him and say
his song was great, but who's he kidding
if he thinks he's going to make it?

sure, he can have your last cigarette.
isn't that song sweet, that chorus line of

fuck it all, come with me.
put those banknotes to the breeze,
to the first empty cup on the high street.

fuck the suits and haircuts.
fuck the upper-middle classes.
fuck working for the weekends.
follow me.

it begins outside, under the orange glow of a
lamp post while god smokes like he's been doing it
since fifteen. your ted baker suit a black stain in
a crowd of charity shop jumpers and hand-me-down
boots. they're saying *what, him?*

and god says *yeah, him.*

philip

'and all ate and were filled.'

mark 6:42

you drive the van, picking up and dropping off cardboard boxes,
                          plastic crates, shopping bags,
          slender, trembling hands; passing thanks from
          dry, hissing lips.

at the table he lists, sorts, assembles: tins, packets, bottles,
oh so quiet, no show but clipboard tallies,
          chews his own flesh as he thinks: *how much? how many?*

there's a mathematics to hunger:
     four children, two parents, seven days, seven something
per hour, one meal,
     five school days – month broken down into minutes.

and you know it keenly, your childhood measured
in slices of bread,
individual grains of rice –   *why would they have them*
                                     if they can't feed them?

infinite love in their counting, hope stitched across the gaps of
your tables,
praying for kisses made edible.

you unload the bounty:
               a tin of beans, a bag of pasta, a bar of chocolate –
a feast of potential and he marks it down twice, three times,
fifty, five hundred.

          each time it's placed in a parcel, still it remains on the
food bank table,
          waiting there, waiting in the box, waiting on the shelf,
waiting in his hands:

one sausage turned a week's worth of breakfasts,
a mars bar no longer to be shared, but one each, for every kid:
some quiet miracle filling bellies
not with fairy food or stone soup but something real.

and you watch, astounded,
yet knowing that the problem with maths
is it just keeps going
just like he does, exhausted, mumbling his mantra:

i'll feed them,
i'll feed them.

bartholomew

'get up. pick up your mat and walk.'

john 5:8

hardest of all is rising,
    always done unseen –
              this blanket, heavy as the earth,
          pressed down upon your body.
some days
       to pull it back is to peel off your own skin.

               and philip, kindest friend, so unfailingly
            offers up his arm to lift
                even your name, clumsy,
             tacked on beside his,
           holds you through every step
              until your legs buckle beneath you,
           your own weight impossible.

hasn't there been some mistake?
              you ask god, down on your knees.
        it's not too late to choose again –
                    i'm no sampson.

he gives no answer.
his eyes upon you as you press your hand to the ground
                   and rise again.

jude

'he will rescue them from oppression and violence,
for precious is their blood in his sight.'

psalm 72:14

and here's the *god hates fags* brigade,
bumping against you, hoping to topple you,
hands grazed against the concrete,
bring you down, low and humble.

thad,

they're smirking,

*thad, my lad, what're you doing
running round dressed like that?*

– all pink and florals,
floating sleeves and
draping skirts.
jude, you seethe through clenched teeth

while they remind you how burning tarmac reeks,
how falling bricks send up clouds of dust,
how cities crumble
(because you kiss boys;
because you rouge your cheeks when
you're feeling brave enough).

their hands curl into fists,
laughter threaded in their throats
because their wrath is not
the deadliest of sins,

it's your rainbow-painted fingernails.
*ain't jesus ever
teach you that?*

you're screeching,
take his name out of your filthy mouth!

17

your blood on the pavement when they scatter,
when blurred arms bear you down to the river
to wash their stains from your skin,

healing crackling over broken cheekbone,
swollen eye, split lip.

sister, i am with you.

he's never once called you thaddeus.
seen your naked body – seen the woman
with her flat chest, the limp flesh between her legs.
seen perfection.

he presses a tender kiss against your forehead.
sister, there's no such thing as lost causes.

john

'jesus wept.'

john 11:35

in the night, his body is warm as any man's.
you place your ear to his chest listening for thunder,
for birdsong, for a newborn screaming, and hear
only his heart beating steady; slow, soft breath.

it's so easy to love him like this – fingers and mouth,
voice and vision, present beside you –

but this morning you watched lazarus climb out
of the earth. *beloved.* all rot and spasms. *beloved.*
colour seeping back into skin. *beloved.* because
his god commands it, this god here in the bed,

and there's something in his eyes already broken –
like time stretched taut and snapped.

if you ask me to die for you, i'll do it.
if i ask you to survive for me, can you do it?
in the next room, lazarus sits so violently awake,
so unfamiliar, like he left the man in his grave.

how foolish it seems to pray, and yet still you whisper,
don't ask me to. god, don't ask me to.

judas

'judas, is it with a kiss you are betraying the son of man?'
luke 22:47

it's figs you can taste on his lips when you cover his
ears with your hands and become the sell-out of the century.
just you and him awake now – so you step over peter in the
foetal position, john sleeping with his arm thrown across his
eyes, and for every breath you've despised mary, it's you
turning tricks at this hour with crumpled bank notes stuffed
in your back pocket, hot enough to brand the skin through
denim. (and later you'll ask yourself what he asked: *did it have
to be a kiss?* the answer: no. they'd have paid so much more
for greater sins.)

so you thread yourself through the chaos of
fistfights and handcuffs with a mouthful of stolen holiness
staining a purple line on your teeth, ready for you to brush
away in the morning, staring into your own unforgiving eyes.
already the money is worth less and the skin is peeling faster
than chapstick can fix – the headlines: *watch jesus christ and
judas iscariot lock lips!* you hardly recognise your features,
distant, grainy, indistinct beside an old mugshot, hair full of
glitter, face black and blue.

but there it is, the document of the deed –
comments underneath: *dya think hes fucked em all?* (and you
breathe coffee and aspirin straight into your lungs, hack it up
over the keyboard. the answer: no. not you, never you.) isn't
that what this is all about? out on the lake with peter; beloved
fucking john; mary's hands kneading his bare feet. *well c soon
enuff.* there he is, like you wanted, god on trial: solicitation,
incitement, evasion, possession, resistance; at the mercy of the
state.

when does it stop?
designer cologne seeps into the rot of the floorboards. you
stand in the doorway, frozen under his gaze as his pupils shrink

down into pinpricks. mary's knees scrape against the floor in front of him, his hands tangled in her dark hair as she moves, the two of them enveloped in the thick haze. *there will always be poor. i am finite.*

your tears are hot on your face like molten silver and the barrel sits heavy on your tongue, tastes like blood. (they asked you for the price of a kiss. you didn't know it.)

james the less

'is this not the carpenter's son? is not his mother called mary? and are not his brothers james and joseph and simon and judas?'

matthew 13:55

you look just like him.

in the mirror you compare yourself,
    turning and twisting.
                    is it in the jaw,
        the brow?

both of you brown as your mother:
    hair, eyes, skin,
        but in you something lacks,
     something missing.

                downstairs, she's wailing
      into john's chest
        while you rinse your brother's blood
                into the sink,
      watch it drain into nothingness
as the crowd pounds at the door,
    tell us more, tell us more
           rattling in their open locust mouths,
  hungering,

    your baby photos, not enough –
        school reports, not enough –
        his mangled body, not enough.

           what's a statement worth?
      trussed up in your darkest suit,
         reading from a paper under flashing bulbs:

it is with great sadness we announce the death
           of a man who liked a sugar in his coffee,

who gently caught spiders and took them outside,
who tucked six siblings in at night,
and ask for privacy at this time.

no, let howling silence say
you'll never fucking know him.

mary magdalene

'do not grieve. be brave;
his grace is always with you to guard you.'
                        the gospel according to mary magdalene

                    at the burial, they discover
                            you sing 'ave verum'
                        just as sweet as joy division,
            voice wishing for resurrection
                like a sudden apparition of birds,
                like forgiveness,
                like baby's breath grown among the gravestones
                            and digitalis.

andrew's hand
    strokes over the swell of your belly.

who sired the bastard babe-to-be?
        they catcall in the streets,
    but before all else the child is yours.
even god's son raised him higher,
    better than he could have been before.

                                        whore.

                when they speak of broken things, they speak of
                japanese pottery, grounded doves, hearts –
                        never the creak of a bedroom door,
                    bruises worn like pearls, everything you have
                        shoved in an overnight bag.

                        wicked woman, witch,
                            cursed, possessed, lain with the devil,
                            temptation in a too-short skirt –

but what of wicked fathers? wicked husbands?

you were dark-eyed and drunken;
yelling your sins from the top of your lungs;
divorced and dancing
under god's gaze. he might have played guitar
but you, bravest among them, banged the drum.

and now alone again in the gardens, always,
earthly delight, prayers for heaven,
paradise, first wild, now withered.
falling's such a heady scent.
you light another cigarette;
shed eyeliner tears for happy endings,
saviours
and the girl worth saving.

he promised these things weren't your fault
but it doesn't feel like it.
he promised. he promised.

woman, why are you weeping?
who do you seek?

you kiss his cheeks, his temples,
press your face into his neck, run your fingers
through his hair, earth in every fold.

don't be surprised.
it was you who taught me how to rise
from the pit they dug for me.

thomas

*'sustain me according to your word, that i may live; and do
not let me be ashamed of my hope.'*

psalm 119:116

in retrospect, there are stranger things, but
you've a scientist's brain and their ecstatic gasping
wasn't beyond reasonable doubt:
how they stumbled over their own stories;
how words like *miracle* were bandied about so carelessly.
so you fell back upon empiricism – didn't state conclusively
anything other than you'd need to see for yourself.

you're no cynic, but you do know the bite
of disappointment: your father's voice slurring,
next weekend, next weekend, down the telephone
and the promise never kept;
the jaws of hope untethered like a dog off its lead
sinking its teeth in despite the doctors saying,
there's nothing more we can do; not if, but when,
reality hangs limp from the worst possibility, limp and dead,
already mouldering in the afternoon's sickly light –
those days of suffocation behind locked doors,
wincing at sirens, waiting for the knock,
for the dread of your name being called.

and still, here he is despite all you've ever learnt.
hold these bloodied wrists.
feel the warmth of my flesh.
count the beat of my pulse.
i'm not leaving. i'm never leaving.

simon peter

'and on this rock i will build my church.'

matthew 16:18

and here's paxman's question:
do you deny it?

all the lies about the fish?
you do deny them.
the deck sinking beneath your feet,
their limbless, flailing bodies
gasping, struggling, panic,
eyes glazed with ignorance
as you threw them back by the armful
to save them, save yourself.
the eu had nothing to do with it,
only his hands grazing yours in the slime,
his laughter as the boat rocked,
assured of something you were not.

he rolls his eyes behind his cue cards:
but do you deny it?

reports that you stood on the surface of the water?
you do deny them.
they call you stone for a reason,
he the first of them, his hand light upon your cheek
where your own touch is heavy, earthbound,
like your feet of clay
the moment you met the surface of the lake
and broke its tension.
the far-right say someone else
pulled you onto the land;
why should their nation bear the weight?
let germany take you if it would make them.

must i ask you again, simon,
if you deny it?

sweating in your seat beneath the studio light,
what else is there to do but to deny him?
the wine of love turned back to water
in your mouth as you drown
beneath the sea of waiting gazes
as they shift and murmur,
cough into their closed fists. say,
like a brother, like a mentor, like a friend.
i never knew if he were god,
if he meant everything he said,
or if he intended anything for rome.
what else is left?

so he relents,
does not ask again,

enough to see the poor man dead,
the union folding like a pack of cards
collapsing, falling on your head, your shoulders,
and you washed up,
sitting, driftwood, on an italian beach
watching dinghies and rowboats on the horizon.
his hand is upon you again,
at your elbow when you turn to look
into the rising sun, into his face.
do you love me, peter?
say again, again, again, *yes, always.*
follow his arm out towards those capsizing ships.

good.
i told you that i would make you a fisher of men.

james the great

what they'll forget to say is they hated you before all this:

hated the span of your hands,
　　　　hated the deep baritone of your voice,
　　　　　　　the bones of your ancestors,
　　　　　　　　　foundations of your home,
prayers on the lips of your mother, your skin in the sun,
your guts,

and they only ever needed half a reason,
　　　　　　　　　　　　less.
they'll spill the contents of your pockets before the court,
　　　　another filthy criminal, but nowhere in the holy law
　　　　　　　　does god say *thou shalt not imbibe* –
　　　　possession is not numbered among deadly sins.

yet still you're fit to die.
　　　　and die you will like god did:

　　　　your arms spread against the sky,
　　　　　　crying, *i am not resisting you.*

but there's a thunder thrumming
　　　　in your veins as the crowd draws near,
　　　　　　spectators to the lightning in your dark eyes,
　　　　　　　　waiting to see what happens next.
does this god of yours lift a finger to intervene?
do you ascend in glorious light?

no, you'll lie where you fell,
　　　　face down in the tarmac,

lead in those last few painful breaths,
shoot the dog before it reaches the courthouse steps.

　　　　so afraid,
　　　　　　so desperately afraid.

acknowledgements

poems in this pamphlet, some in an earlier form, have previously appeared in the following journals: *algebra of owls*, *BARNHOUSE*, *ghost city review*, *the high window*, *pigeonholes*, *prole*, *strix* and *8 poems*. thank you very much to all their editors. the poem 'philip' was also shortlisted for the leeds peace poetry prize 2018, with thanks to head judge simon armitage.

many thanks to the following, without whom this body of work would not have been possible: my family, the nerd herd, renaissance, christopher bowles, kate garrett, pete green, sam grudgings, bob horton, kit rayne and rebecca roy.

matthias

'you believe because you have seen.
blessed are those who have not seen, and yet believe.'
john 20:29

and who are you, matthias?
  or, as right, who am i?

patron saint of the chronically late,
  everyone who ever blinked and missed it.
 some maniac's prayer,
   some caricature of madness.

(perhaps it's true.
  there's no god left here to whisper in your ear.)

but when peter drew your name from the hat
  up you jumped from your seat, no questions asked
 of why the lot should fall to you;
   after all, apostles are not born but called
    to bear the neck,
     sign on for death.

(the bread of heaven
  is human flesh, faith a currency,
 and starving rats eat anything;
   thieves' hands take fistfuls from your pockets.)

your request:
   love take my mouth, let me beat my breast
    and speak you into being.
hope take my hands, let me call out
   and build a new temple, better than before –
  not of bank balances and birds in cages but
   banquet halls and dancefloors.

i believe in the world not as i've seen it
 but as it could be. listen, you gathered here,
    and let me tell you a story about a god.
     let me tell you a story about a man.